"The Secret Keys *are an invaluable tool for seasoned Direct Mailers or newcomers. It outlines Best Practices and can save you significant time and money. Thank you Rainer!"*

-Debbie Major, Data Direct Group Inc.

"If you're reading this, you're holding a production 'Bible'. It contains countless valuable tips and tricks of the trade compiled by the man who, literally and figuratively, wrote the book on DM production."

-Bob Knight, R. J. Knight & Associates

"Many suppliers claim they'll truly be your "partner." But very few get to know your business as well as Rainer does. Fewer still can provide efficient solutions to your needs. Working with him makes me look good!"

-Gilles Roy, Gilles Roy & Associates

"The 10 Keys of Successful Direct Mail Production" *is a very useful guide to making sure that your DM campaigns are properly executed and delivered on time. Well worth reading, keeping on hand and passing on to the newbies in the business. Sage words and very practical advice; something of good value to all DM practitioners, from production to creative people."*

-Michael Hofmann, Resource Mail Services

"Too often we spend our time and energy on the upfront work in Direct Mail, only to see it fall apart because we didn't take care of the execution. Costs soar and deadlines fall by the wayside when you don't think about how best to put your great ideas into action. Rainer has done a remarkable job of putting together a 'must read' resource for anyone planning their next direct marketing project."

-Janine Foster, St. Lawrence College

"Having been responsible for the production of thousands of direct mail packages, I believe Rainer's Secret Keys *is an excellent manual for DM newbies and pros alike. His clearly-written tips are a superb checklist every mailer can use to avoid common pitfalls, and save time and money.*

-Marlena McCarthy, Done Write Communications

"I found "The 10 Secret Keys To Successful Direct Mail Printing" *to be an excellent source for direct mail professionals at all levels. I've shared it with a few new hires as a great starting point for understanding some of the challenges in our business. Thanks and keep up the good work."*
-Michael L. Vitch, Compu-Mail

"Rainer's book filled with practical points , helped me apply many tips to a completely new area of Hotels and Restaurants that too in India where direct marketing is at a very infancy stage. THANKS Rainer!!"
-Vikram Kamat, Marketing Manager

"Save yourself headaches and thousands of dollars, before you send out your next mailing. Rainer knows what he's talking about, read this book today."
-Ray Khan, Khan Scope Centre

THE 10
SECRET KEYS
TO
SUCCESSFUL
DIRECT MAIL
PRINTING

Rainer Fischer

DM Graphics Inc.

ISBN: 978-0-9917999-0-9

Dedicated to:
My family & its entourage

Thank You For Purchasing This Book.

Direct mail printing, which encompasses both print and mail services, is generally given little attention in the direct mail marketing community.

Most of the focus is on pre-production efforts, and as a result in many cases, the last steps end up being rushed. It is often assumed that this final execution will go through quickly and efficiently. Too little attention is paid to the lesser-known details of production.

I go into more detail in the back of the book but for now let's just say that direct mail is more than just list, copy and offer. Unless you put some of your focus and energy into looking after the production end of things, your mail campaign could very well end up being a disaster.

Even the simple mailings that seem 'easy' can go astray. That doesn't mean production has to be hard or complicated. It doesn't have to be all that 'hi-tech' either. Just follow the tried-and-proven guidelines that I've described in this book and you'll be well on your way to producing a successful mailing.

Rainer Fischer

**Before You Read The Rest of
This Book, Check Out
A Very Special Direct Mail Offer
That Is Only Available For
A Limited Time!**

http://specialoffer.dmgraphics.ca

Table of Contents

Key 1: Supplying Art To Your Printer

It is always advisable to provide 'native' art in its original design format to the printer. PDF-formatted art does not allow the printer to make *significant* design changes at his end.

Supply your printer with ***native*** art. By 'native' I am not referring to the beautiful aboriginal art created by North American native peoples. I am referring to artwork in its original design format such as *Adobe InDesign* or *QuarkXpress.*

Although the trend nowadays is to supply high resolution (hi-res) art as a PDF (**Portable Document Format**), it is usually not the preferable format for direct mail printing.

Here's why…

In many cases, there are inevitably last-minute changes required in the final art that is supplied by the client. This could range from minor changes like typos to much more critical revisions such as moving graphics or text.

With PDF art, it is not possible to make these changes, and so revised art is then required from the client.

In the case of more advanced revisions, possibly due to dm production requirements, more time may be needed to make the changes. With new proofs and approvals needed, delays start to kick in. By the time a new PDF has been provided, the printer's schedule may require your job to be 'bumped.'

With native art, the printer can make the changes in his own pre-press department.

While additional costs *may* apply depending on the complexity of the revisions, it certainly would be a more efficient and ideal solution than going back for new client art.

Recently, I produced a print job that required new PDF art no less than three times and resulted in a print delay of one week. Had original art been provided, the changes would have quickly been made by the printer and there would have been no delay in the print schedule.

One of the more common revisions that occur on client-supplied final art is the moving of text or graphics on a **shell** letter (pre-printed stock to be used for laser personalization) that will be used as the addressing vehicle. If not designed properly, it is very frequently necessary to make revisions to <u>allow only the address block</u> to appear through the window envelope.

A line of text requesting various donation amounts showing above the donor's name could be a response-killer and should not be showing through the window.

It is especially important to supply native art if you are not using a designer familiar with direct mail (see **Key 10**). This is usually when most, although not all, of these situations occur.

When To Use PDFs

There are definitely steps in the production process where PDFs are very useful. One of these is at the very beginning when <u>jobs are being quoted</u>. As the old saying goes, *"A picture is worth a thousand words."*

PDFs will:

- confirm client specifications

- help to clarify the print requirements since many clients are not familiar with print terminology

- allow for a quick review of the art to ensure that the design complies with postal requirements

- determine if the design meets the most cost-efficient production standards

PDFs are also useful for the printer as:

- a *quick preliminary check* that the art matches the quotation or estimate

- a *preliminary reference* to check against the art

- a *confirmation* for the Purchase Order

PDFs are also useful as *proofs*. Nowadays, on-line proofs sent as an e-mail attachment have become the most popular and convenient method of proofing. On-line proofs have greatly helped in significantly reducing dm timelines.

Even though on-line PDF proofs do not necessarily provide 100% accurate color on a computer monitor, they do nevertheless provide an excellent representation of what will be printed prior to any trimming or bindery.

Other additional methods of proofing, such as hard-copy laser proofs or press approvals, may be necessary but a preliminary PDF proof will allow the printer to go ahead and set up the press. In most cases, the printer will not go ahead unless he has a signed-off preliminary PDF proof.

A Word of Caution: Any changes to artwork at the time of a press check, other than what can be done on the press, will require 'pulling the job' off the press, revising and ripping the new art, making plates and setting up the press again at a later date, all to the tune of hundreds of dollars in additional charges.

Key 2: Print Enough Overs

> **Calculating 'overs' into your print order up front is a cheap insurance policy to allow for lettershop setup and spoilage as well as the occasional printer under-runs. Above all, refuse to work with any printers who specify an 'industry policy of 5% over or under.'**

In my experience, this is one of the most neglected keys in dm production. Nothing is worse than overcoming numerous hurdles and challenges to get the job *almost* complete, and then the lettershop calls to tell you that they've run out of stock!

After a flurry of calls back and forth between you and the lettershop, you and the printer, and then you and the lettershop again, you inevitably find yourself in a no-win situation. The lettershop denies wasting any stock and the printer hotly claims he printed and shipped the correct quantity! What to do?

Now, in a panic situation, you find yourself having to decide between cutting back the mailing quantity in order to meet the mail date and budget, or going 'back on press' at great expense and probably missing the mail date.

You will most certainly not be the most popular person on your marketing team. Even after the job is finally out the door, you will still be dealing with the challenges of bad feelings and bruised relationships, along with the real possibility of unexpected costs.

For the cost of literally a few extra dollars, these scenarios can <u>easily</u> be avoided.

Lettershops are normally able to recycle leftover stock so as to accommodate our environmental concerns. The extra dollars paid out for overs are a well-spent **insurance policy**. Consider it part of your regular production costs. At least that way, you will have a <u>fixed</u> cost right at the outset and no unnecessary costs at the end.

Overs on printed stock should be factored in for <u>any</u> of the following reasons:

- Imaging equipment setup requires stock for both job proofs as well as actual production runs;

- Downstream equipment such as folders, trimmers and inserters require setup stock;

- Clients want completed job samples;

- Printers can also short-ship – yes, they actually do!

Also keep in mind that the imaging, or variable data personalization, process requires *more* overs because of laser setup and spoilage in addition to the other downstream processes. Other non-personalized inserts require slightly less overs.

Note should also be made about expensive specialty items that have required a long lead time to produce. Careful consideration should be given to the number of overs for such pieces. The fraction it will cost to order a few more up front will be well worth the extra insurance to ensure a successful completion of the mailing.

Running short at the nth hour on a special premium insert that took 4 weeks to deliver at great expense could be a disaster. It's safer to tack on a few extra dollars for up-front insurance by ordering extras.

Specialty items that require special finishing like *re-moistenable* glue or *die-cutting* would normally be part of the printer's job. Just be sure to specify to him what your net quantity to the lettershop needs to be – he will factor in overs for his own internal production spoilage. This cost should be reflected in his pricing to you.

How many overs should you allow for?

There is not always a straight-forward answer to this question. Unfortunately, a **percent rule** is difficult to apply because jobs with smaller quantities require a higher percentage of overs compared to a larger run. Percentages can vary from as low as 1% on a large 500,000-piece mailing to 50%, or higher, on a small 1,000-piece item that requires personalization. Then, you also need to consider the difficulty of the stock being personalized.

The following table is a rough guideline for standard stock that I have found handy over the years. Some people however order much more.

Quantity	Personalized	Non-Personalized
Up to 999	500	500
1,000 – 2,999	500	500
3,000 – 3,999	500	500
4,000 – 9,999	1,000	1,000
10,000 – 49,999	2,000	2,000
50,000 – 99,999	3,000	2,000
100,000 - 149,999	4,000	3,000
150,000 - 199,999	4,000	3,000
200,000 – 499,999	5,000	4,000
500,000+	Varies	Varies

If you are dealing directly with a print shop, tell the printer the exact quantity that needs to be delivered to the lettershop, <u>including your overs</u>. Let him know that <u>you will not accept less</u>. Some printers will actually deliver their own overs to your lettershop at no charge. This is a sign of someone who wants your business.

A Word of Caution: *REFUSE* to deal with any printer who quotes the industry 'standard policy of 5% over or under.' You certainly don't want to be short-shipped and at the same time, you also don't want to be billed for any extra long after the job is done. It should be the <u>responsibility of</u>

<u>the printer</u> to build in his own overs and then build it into his price <u>up front</u>.

The only 'extras' should be anything that was not originally quoted. I specified my own policy of '**no over or under**' policy to my own suppliers years ago and it has never been a problem. Printers who want your business will be reasonable.

Key 3: Reduce Your Number of Letter Versions

Increasing the number of versions of offset-printed stock or laser 'shells' increases the risk for error during production. Whenever possible, use 'variable data printing' (VDP), or personalization, to minimize the number of offset-printed versions.

Data mining and segmentation have advanced tremendously since the days of the *cheshire*, or paper address label. However, multi-segmented files can increase the complexity of your printed stock, and in turn, your entire campaign because of the many **pre-printed versions** that may be required to accommodate the personalized data.

In order to increase response rates nowadays, it is necessary to segment and personalize the various groups within your lists using the relational data that has been gathered about them. The personalization may involve just a different paragraph, or it could even be a signature by different department managers.

Mailings can be sophisticated in their segmentation and personalization but it doesn't mean that they cannot be <u>simple</u> for production purposes.

Sometimes it can get too complicated. I was once asked to quote on a job that required more than 400 different pre-printed back pages of a personalized letter! I politely declined since the tremendous cost to go through 400 plates and setups for printing the stock as well as the enormous risk of keeping track of 400 different stocks at the lettershop far outweighed the costs to just laser print the back pages.

Here's another example: A mailing is comprised of laser-personalized letters coming from 100 different branches or chapters of an organization, each with a completely different signature. Should the client ask his printer to print 100 versions of the letter to accommodate all the signatures?

Imagine the potential for error when the lettershop is required to keep track of 100 different stock versions!

How could this be handled more cost-effectively in a more secure environment?

In this example, the simplest and most cost-effective method is to laser-personalize (or inkjet) the different branches and signatures. If it is done correctly, only <u>ONE</u> version of laser stock is required. Very simple, very clean.

The return address of the appropriate branch for each name, or record, can simply be laser-printed above the recipient's name and address at the beginning of the letter. The branch address is positioned in such a way that it will show through the <u>top window of a double-window</u> outer envelope when the letter is finally folded down and inserted. In this way, the recipient sees that the letter is coming from his or her own branch.

For the signatures, it is only a matter of the lettershop scanning in hard copies of each participant's handwritten signature (black ink is best) and then linking them back to the corresponding branches. When the letter is being laser-personalized, both the branch and signature will be automatically pulled into the letter for each record.

If it happens that the signature ends up on the back side because of the length of the letter copy, rather than pre-print shells with 100 different signatures, you will still be much better off using duplex-laser. It will be much safer. Even if it costs a little more (compare printer and lettershop pricing), it is better to err on the side of <u>simplicity</u>. In fact, it may well end up being the most *inexpensive* solution compared to using 100 versions and something goes wrong.

Another time when you should consider just laser-printing and not pre-printing is when you need to laser into a specific area onto the sheet with pin-point accuracy. Examples are when you need to drop variable dollar amounts into a small box or boxes.

Because trimming of sheets may not always be accurate, the final destination of your dollar arrays may not line up properly with the rest of the pre-printed graphics. (Note: even 1/16" can make a difference),.

Therefore, consider laser-printing any small check boxes or graphics as well as the dollar amounts. Your laser shop should be able to produce these small graphics for you.

If you want to keep your stock even simpler, you could consider using <u>blank</u> stock and going with *digital printing* or *imaging* using 4-color toner or inks. In this type of application, complete images, graphics and text can be personalized on an individual basis. The more expensive pricing of these jobs still puts it out of the reach of most mailers, although the cost of this application is gradually decreasing.

Financial institutions, car manufacturers and other *Fortune 500* corporations with large budgets seem to be the prime users of this more advanced technology.

You can also use blank stock and go completely in-line for all of your production including printing, personalization and even envelope construction. This type

---

Laser It All!

Many people think it's cheaper to laser only the name and address on a letter.

In reality, laser shops charge *by the sheet*, not by the amount of toner used. So, for the same price, it's always best to laser-print the *whole letter*.

The only exception would be if you are using **a lot** of detailed color within the letter copy itself and you are paying for only a black laser job. In that case, either pre-print the entire page with all its colors, or go with full-color imaging.

---

of package is run on a very large, very specialized piece of equipment which is usually not financially feasible on jobs less than a couple of hundred thousand pieces. You are also limited to a particular type of package design.

This format is also quite useful for personalizing premiums or involvement inserts that normally cannot be personalized on regular types of laser or inkjet printers.

Please Note: If you do end up with more than one version of pre-printed stock or shells, insist that your printer label the different versions very clearly on not only the <u>outside of every box</u> but also to list them <u>on the Packing Slip</u>. Details on the Packing Slip should include the number of boxes, quantity per box and the total quantity of each version.

Key 4: Minimize The Cost of Personalization

You can keep your imaging costs down by pre-printing (offset print) non-personalized areas of your letter. These areas include multiple pages and special techniques such as colored text, underlining, signatures and handwritten notes.

Having discussed the merits of personalization rather than offset printing, I'd like to switch tracks and talk about the benefits of offset printing versus laser printing.

If your mailing is fairly simple with maybe one to three versions of the letter, it is best to keep unnecessary imaging to a minimum and save yourself some dollars.

The most common example of this minimization of imaging is the back side of the letter. In most direct mail packages that include a personalized letter, the length of the letter usually extends to two or more pages. Unless page 2 and subsequent pages contain variable data information, these pages can be pre-printed but it's important that the look of ALL the pages is the same, with the **font** being the major consideration.

We can do this with a little-used technique called **font-matching**. Our company developed it many years ago to enhance the **personalization effect** that variable data printing creates. If you just use the letter text that is created within the artwork, there *may* still be noticeable differences in ink and toner appearances.

I have used this technique for many years with much success and although it is not as critical as it was when **Courier** was the font of choice, it nevertheless helps to give that little extra bit of personalization and authenticity to your letter.

Although most consumers understand the concept of 'one-on-one' mass communication, there is still the 'hidden magic' of a highly personalized piece of mail. After mailing tens of millions of direct mail pieces for clients over the years, it still awes me when a consumer or donor comments on his or her *personal* letter.

Direct mail personalization works! And anything we can do to enhance that effect will only make your mailing MORE successful!

So while this font-matching technique may seem like a lot of extra work for little in return, think again about the personalized letters that you receive and your own reaction to the letter. Besides copy and offer, what else made you react positively?

RAINER FISCHER

It was the small, hidden details behind the scene that did their magic.

The idea behind this technique is to make sure that the back pre-printed side of the sheet will MATCH <u>exactly</u> the laser-printed personalized version on the front. The only way that this can happen is if the back page is printed using the <u>same laser printer</u> as will be used on the front side.

How To Match The Front And Back Page Fonts

First, have the lettershop or laser shop print out a hard copy of the final, client-approved version of the back page(s) on the identical laser printer that will be running the job. This is important – it <u>must be the same laser printer</u> that will be running the actual job.

Next, the printer uses a high-resolution camera to 'shoot' the hard copy, makes film and plate, and then puts it on the press with the rest of the artwork. It is then offset printed.

When it is finally laser-printed and personalized, the front page of the letter will match the pre-printed back page making it appear that the letter was run on someone's personal office printer. *Voilà* – a completely personalized letter!

There are times when you may want to add a little more appeal to your letter with colored headlines, underlines, signatures or handwritten notes. This normally is not a problem unless you want to do it on a page with *variable data personalization.*

Instead of paying for more expensive full-color imaging, you can do this using only a black laser printer and an experienced laser shop!

Laser-printing onto shells with special colored graphics, especially underlines, requires a lot of skill and it has to be accurate to look authentic. The same applies if you need to laser-print beside colored boxes or graphics, or in small, tight areas.

If the lettercopy has been correctly formatted within the artwork, it is just a matter of printing only the colored areas (underlines, signatures, notes, etc.) onto the shells, omitting the actual letter text which will laser-personalized.

If, however, the lettercopy has not yet been formally laid out because you are leaving it up to your laser shop to do that for you, then your printer will need to work with a hard copy of the letter, including the underlined areas.

Using a printer's light table, he can trace the underlines (usually done in a handwritten-style) onto a blank piece of paper using a black pen or marker. Similar to the font-matching technique I described earlier, the printer captures the image with a high-resolution camera, makes film and plate, and adds it to the press.

This part must be done very carefully and accurately so that the underlines will be positioned correctly when printed. Keep in mind that underlines are not designed to be used with *variable data text* because you have no control of the pre-printed underlines at this point and therefore cannot shorten or extend them to match the variable data.

A Couple of Extra Notes: You should also double-check that you are offset printing postal indicias, especially on window envelopes, since they cannot be run through the high heat of laser printers.

Also, remember that when you are offset printing the additional pages of the letter, have the printer ship them <u>flat</u> to the lettershop. The lettershop will fold them along with the personalized first sheet at the same time – this will ensure that they will <u>fold together</u> properly.

Key 5: Make Sure That The Lettershop Can Run Your Stock

> **Be careful what stock you plan to use for your direct mail campaign. It must be compatible for both the imaging equipment as well as the downstream insertion machines. The wrong stock can cause expensive delays and reprints.**

One of the most heart-sinking phone calls during a direct mail campaign is one that says that the stock you just printed at great expense and was just shipped to your lettershop, is unusable! These last-minute problems can make or break your campaign because of additional costs or a missed mail drop, or both.

Unexpected printing or lettershop costs can put your campaign into a loss situation quite easily. Since many direct mail jobs are integrated with other media marketing, a delayed mail drop can have serious repercussions.

Believe it or not, in my experience, it's a <u>frequent</u> problem!

Therefore, it is important that you have someone in your corner who understands production and will keep an eye open for potential problems – and there are certainly many when it comes to dm stock.

If you are not using a supplier who is managing your entire campaign from print to mail delivery at the postal processing plant, you are leaving yourself open to serious coordination issues. You should use either an experienced dm art designer (see **Key 10**) or printer (see **Key 9**) who will flag problems <u>before</u> stock is printed and delivered to your lettershop.

If he is unsure about machine specs at your lettershop, a knowledgeable printer will check with your lettershop <u>before</u> stock is printed. If necessary, stock should be tested for laser or insertion compatibility <u>before any stock is ordered or printing is done</u>.

Whether you are running a job in-line using continuous laser imaging or using sheet-fed lasers, you should be aware of stocks and additional processes that cause production issues.

Here is a list of some of them:

- Use only **wax-free inks** on any stock that will be laser-imaged. Laser printers produce tremendous heat that will literally melt any wax on the sheet resulting in a smeary, inky mess!

- Do not use **offset spray powder** on any stock that will be running on laser printers. Offset powder is used by some printers to speed up the drying process, especially on high ink coverage pieces. The fine white particles of the powder (similar to baby powder) accumulate inside the laser printers causing misfeeds and damage to the inner workings of the laser printers.

- Use only **micro-perforations** on any laser stock. Micro-perfs are applied on the printing press rather than on a folder, and do not leave behind a perforation 'ridge.' These ridges will cause misfeeds on the sheet-fed laser printers, sometimes up to 10 sheets at a time. The general rule of thumb: if you can feel it with your fingers, then there is a good chance that it will cause feeding problems on the laser.

- Make sure that any additional **paper coatings** are heat-resistant. This applies to any re-moistenable glue applications as well as varnish and aqueous coatings (AQ). If the recipient is to use a pen to complete any response form, make sure that these areas are free of varnish (spot varnish). Normally, spot AQ cannot be applied but check with your printer before ruling it out – it can be done.

- Use only **stock sizes and weights** that are compatible with the imaging equipment. Most imaging equipment maxes out at 12" x 18" or 14" x 17" while some can only handle the standard sizes of 8-½" x 11", 8-½" x 14" and 11" x 17". (See **Key 6**). Most imaging equipment can handle stock weights up to 10-pt weight and some can handle heavier weights. By far, the most common stock is 60 lb offset or 24 lb bond paper for sheets and 24 lb whitewove for envelopes.

- **Grain direction** of the stock can be an issue for laser or lettershop production. Check with your lettershop.

- Use only laser-friendly versions of **textured stock**. Otherwise the laser toner will not adhere properly.

- Any **special bindery** processes must be carefully reviewed to make sure that the piece can pass through a laser printer, or that it can even be used on insertion equipment. Such processes can include re-moistenable gluing, die-cutting, kiss-cutting, folding and tipping.

It is a wise policy to check with your lettershop on any of its equipment specs, or at the very least, ask your printer to check it out when he is still quoting you a price and before he gets your job.

Key 6: Avoid Last-Minute Problems

An excellent way to avoid costly delays is to take advantage of the expertise of your production suppliers prior to the actual production by having them sit in on design sessions.

A lot of last-minute problems can be avoided by simply including your production at the <u>beginning</u> of your campaign.

Once you have a preliminary format of your direct mail package designed, or even <u>prior to creating a budget</u> for your campaign, you can invite them to sit down with your design and strategy teams to discuss various production options and costs.

As a matter of fact, serious consideration should be given to inviting both your printer and your lettershop to these meetings.

This is especially important if your designer is new to direct mail. I have been to many meetings where the art directors were, in fact, veteran dm designers. It just means that more options can be brought up and discussed.

As in any industry, new and improved technologies are constantly being developed in the dm field.

Just as designers have their own new technologies to keep track of, so can the production team bring new ideas to the table.

Yes, your printer can certainly be contacted and meet with you later in your schedule to discuss options but wouldn't it make more sense to have everyone sit down at the same time to ask questions and be able to make logical decisions based on immediate responses? In the end, you will be saving time and money.

If a mock-up has been created by the design team, it can be reviewed by members of your production team, particularly the printer and lettershop reps.

Remember, printing is a centuries-old trade with a long-standing history. There is probably more than one way to resolve a printing issue. It is better to ask the experts than to try to second-guess a particular issue that can very easily result in unnecessary costs or even worse, a last-minute reprint.

The same rationale should be applied to a job that requires **variable data printing**. Not all lettershops carry the same equipment. Not all will be able to provide the same services; some may not specialize in the type of service that your campaign requires.

For example, some shops are only able to laser the standard sheet sizes of 8-½ x 11, 8-½ x 14 and 11 x 17 while others can run sizes up to 14-1/3 x 20-½ with the newer machines. Continuous form machines can run 14" x 18" which allows for 2-up 8-1/2" x 14." Some shops can also set up their equipment to laser odd sizes. More information on selecting the most appropriate supplier can be found in **Key 8.**

Sample input from printers can include:

- Advice on stock selection based on cost

- Varnish or aqueous coating (AQ) on your full-color job

- 'Print & convert' or 'jet' envelope printing?

- 4-color process or 3/3, and… which is cheaper?

- Advice on special bindery like die-cutting, kiss-cutting, perforations

- Stock samples for testing by the lettershop

The ideal format for your direct mail package will depend a lot on your <u>budget</u> and your <u>target market</u>.

What Kind of Pre-Production Advice Can Your Lettershop Provide You?

Lettershops can advise you on:

- Money-saving postal strategies

- Deliverability requirements

- How to lay out your letter and response to maximize personalization

- How to minimize insertion costs, especially for matching components

- Timelines required to meet your mail date

- Optional package formats

- And much, much more…

In my own experience, I have found that jobs that integrated a meeting of designers and production people *prior to creating final art* flowed through the production process much more smoothly than those that did not. Timelines were not strained and mail dates were more easily met. In addition, production costs were minimized due to valuable pre-production input from suppliers. Design costs were also kept to a minimum because of less re-work.

It's obvious to see, there are many advantages to these types of preliminary pre-production meetings.

Key 7: Make Sure You Have Enough 'Buffer' Time

Scheduling the proper amount of time in your timetable for production will allow for the necessary quality control and 'buffer' time to accommodate unexpected delays.

Too many times, to the detriment of the entire campaign, too little time is left to complete the actual production, for <u>both</u> printing and lettershop. Very often, direct mail managers consider the campaign 'as good as done' once the strategy has been laid out, lists selected and artwork completed.

Nothing could be riskier!

While it is nice to know that you can count on your loyal and valuable production partners to complete the job on time, sometimes even in record time, anything can happen when things are rushed!

Great printers can make mistakes. Great lettershops can make mistakes. Even great dm designers and managers can make mistakes.

When deciding on a supplier, there is no sense in looking for one who doesn't make any mistakes – your best guideline is to find the one who makes the ***least mistakes!*** Anyone can make mistakes and if enough 'buffer' time isn't allowed to correct them, the campaign can suffer as a result.

Years ago, in the pre-email days and even going back to the pre-fax days, 4 weeks was an acceptable turnaround time for printing followed by another couple of weeks for lettershop, depending of course on the volume being mailed.

Nowadays it is not uncommon for clients to request a weekend turnaround on printing or mailing services.

While it certainly can be done, it is never a wise move to push your suppliers to the wall on a regular basis. It is only a matter of time before they will resent the intrusion on family time. Save the special favors for the <u>real</u> emergencies!

Most mistakes happen during times of stress caused by *lack of time*. Quality control (QC) checks will be skipped – and you know that the one QC step skipped will be that one step that would have been the key in catching the problem!

Most production companies create their most effective QC systems based on past problems, meaning that they are there <u>for a reason</u>. Forcing a supplier to skip them because of undue pressure to complete the job in an unreasonable amount of time is never a good strategy.

If you are strapped for time and feel the urge to cut back on your QC, keep in mind the maxim below. Better yet, cut it out and post it right in front of you where it will be a constant reminder:

> **"There is <u>always time</u> to do it right the <u>second time!</u>"**

Even though the job may initially move through the printing stage quickly, it can be difficult, if not impossible, for the last supplier in the queue to deliver the job on time. I have witnessed countless times when the job was missed being delivered to the post office because the lettershop could have used <u>just one more hour</u>!

It may seem this is common sense and an unnecessary point make, but it has been my experience that it needs to be a constant reminder. It is important to allow a reasonable amount of time to complete the dm production <u>properly</u>. Discuss with your printer and lettershop well in advance how much time they need to do the job.

No doubt they will factor in 'buffer' time which will allow for some unexpected <u>minor</u> setbacks such as revised art, delayed approvals, equipment breakdowns, late deliveries, etc. Remember, too, that you are not the only client (surprise!) and sometimes your job will need to be 'bumped' if the delays are created at your end.

Key 8: Use The Best Vendor For YOUR Job

Selecting the most appropriate supplier for your job is one of the most, if not <u>the</u> most, important parts of the production process. Building a solid relationship with the ideal supplier will ensure that your 'dream' jobs will not turn into nightmares.

Believe it or not, there are still people trying to fit a square peg into a round hole, either because they are trying to save a few dollars, or trying to be too loyal to their supplier at the wrong times.

Having what looked like a great deal in the beginning when the job was quoted suddenly doesn't look so great anymore when the job is botched, or gets out the (lettershop) door days, and sometimes, *weeks* late.

By sheer number, the choice of printing companies must rank right up there with restaurants. From small 'print-in-my-garage' printers to huge 'where's-my-job' conglomerates, printers offer a wide range of products and services. Most specialize in a particular type of print job based on the equipment that they have on their floor.

The most important factor is to select a printer based on his direct mail experience, <u>not</u> based on his price (see **Key 9**). The more experience he has with dm printing, the greater the chances that your job will not be derailed.

Budget can be a factor, especially if you work in the *Not-For-Profit*, or charity, sector.

In such cases, when you would really like to work with a particular printer, have a talk with him and see if you can negotiate a better price. Perhaps, if your policy allows it, you can promise him the rest of the year's mailings and get a <u>volume discount</u>.

Because of the competitive nature of printing, you will literally find dozens of ads and flyers advertising the lowest prices on everything from envelopes to 4-color brochures. For time-sensitive, more complex direct mail packages, these are not the ideal printers, especially if you are looking for some extra hand-holding and customer service.

If your printer and lettershop are two different companies, try to select them based on their geography if possible. Any savings you may have initially realized may suddenly disappear when shipping the printed pieces halfway across the country.

The Factors To Consider When Selecting A Supplier

Here are the main points to consider before making your final choice:

- **Does the printer have the right equipment for your job?**

  Some printers are set up to run 24/7 printing 4-color process, resulting in prices that are *more* competitive than running a 3-color **PMS (Pantone Matching System) or spot colors**.

  A larger run (over 50,000) with a lot of additional bindery features such as perforations, in-line gluing, varnish, etc. will probably be much more cost-effective running on an in-line web press rather than a sheet-fed press which will require more expensive off-line bindery.

- **Does the lettershop have the equipment to handle your job?**

  There are many types of imaging equipment available on the market today. These machines can include anything from on-line inkjet addressing on the low end to off-line full-color digital imaging on the high end.

  While the majority of laser personalization is still done using black toner, the price of full-color has gradually decreased enough over the past few years that it is now becoming more widely available.

Another consideration should also be the type of **matching** technology that the lettershop is using on its insertion equipment. Unless your job is really not machineable, i.e. the package components will not fit the physical specifications of the inserter, any matching requirements should be *automated* to decrease the cost and *increase the accuracy*.

Hand-matching or hand insertion should <u>always</u> be the last resort because <u>people make mistakes</u>! You should have <u>reasonable expectations</u> if your job is being done manually.

Matching technology has become quite sophisticated over the years. Automated matching codes can range from the more conspicuous bar codes, 2-D bar codes and numbers to the more inconspicuous dots and name recognition software.

Decide which one is right for you based on cost and accuracy. It's always to get samples and take a tour of the operation while jobs are in progress prior to making a final choice.

- **Does the lettershop have the expertise to handle your job?**

Aside from the proper imaging equipment, it is important to select a lettershop that has the necessary expertise to handle your data preparation. It is just as important that they have the knowledge and software to take advantage of all the postal classifications to allow for maximum deliverability of your mail at minimal postal rates.

If they have programmers on staff to handle custom data requests rather than just 'push button' technology, this will be a big benefit if your job has a lot of variable data.

- **Can the supplier handle your volume?**

  While this may seem obvious, some mailers still overlook the fact that a shop that is set up to run jobs up to 20,000 pieces and then demand that the shop process a 100,000-piece mailing in the same time frame. If you insist on using your favorite but smaller shop, then by all means allow them the additional time to complete the job properly. In the end, **you** will suffer most if the mailing derails.

Here are a few other factors to consider when selecting your most appropriate supplier:

- Have past jobs been completed <u>on time</u>?

- Have past jobs been completed <u>accurately</u>?

- Is your Customer Service Rep knowledgeable? Is he/she easy to reach? Is he/she easy to work with?

- Does the supplier have a poor financial history – or have you heard rumblings in the dm community?

- Does the supplier outsource any part of his services?

- Will you use the supplier in the future?

Here is one other great under-used idea: Take a tour of your potential supplier's facilities. Take note of the orderliness and cleanliness, or lack thereof, in the shop. A good rule of thumb to remember is that <u>how they take care of their own place is a good indicator of how they will take care of **your** job</u>!

Key 9: Use An Experienced Direct Mail Printer

> Using a printer who is experienced with direct mail production techniques will 'save your bacon' many times over. He will be a valuable partner by preventing minor issues from becoming major mistakes.

This is a BIGGIE.

The direct mail industry is huge. In 2007, over $58 billion in the U.S. and close to $2 billion in Canada was spent on direct mail advertising. Even with the explosion of internet advertising, dm is still expected to grow in 2008. A major chunk of those expenditures is for printing.

In fact, in most cases other than postage, offset printing is the biggest cost in the production process. Is it any wonder that printers have suddenly become mailing 'experts' with the addition of a new VDP printer? Companies like Xerox, HP and Kodak are climbing over themselves promoting their latest hi-tech printers to excited printers trying to capture new market share.

Even without these high-end imaging machines, many printers will target the direct mail market just to get a little share of the printing pie.

To attract new business from the dm market, many of these printers are willing to provide rock-bottom prices. For many mailers, especially in the *Not-For-Profit* segment, the low prices can be very attractive.

The real danger for direct mailers lies not in the quality of the printed pieces but rather in the lack of a dm knowledgebase good enough to prevent a mailing nightmare a few steps down the road in the lettershop process.

The normal routine is for the printer to use artwork provided by the client, provide a proof and then go ahead with the job once approval has been granted. Once the job has been printed as per the signed-back proof, there is usually very little, if anything, that can be done if it turns out that there actually was a problem.

"We printed it properly… pay the invoice, please!"

Ever heard that from your printer before? If you have, you know what I'm talking about. If not, you don't want to hear it!

The printer is most likely quite within his rights to ask for payment. But where does that leave you? Even if your printer's Customer Service Rep is willing to help you out, any additional costs will most likely be charged by the owner, especially since he gave you such a "competitive" price, i.e. there was already very little profit in the job to start with.

After all, they did a proper printing job – and this is important – based on the artwork and approvals they received.

Some Common Printing Mistakes

Over the years, I have seen so many problems like this that it's hard to pick out any particular example. However, let me describe a couple of situations that repeat themselves many times over.

Situation #1: Placing The Window Of The Outer Envelope In The Wrong Position Is Probably One Of The Most Common Mistakes

When using a 6 x 9 (or 5-⅞ x 9 or 5-⅞ x 9-½) outer window envelope, it is important to determine where the window will sit relative to the folded-down addressing vehicle. For example, a standard 8-½ x 11 letter or 8-½ x 14 letter/response is usually folded down to 8-½ x 5-½ for this type of envelope.

Assuming that a standard address layout is used, i.e. the address block is closer to the top of the letter, the envelope window will need to sit much higher up from the standard position of ⅝" from the left and ¾" from the bottom. A window placed 2-¾" from the bottom would be the correct position.

However, a lot of graphics at the top of the letter would change the dynamics once again and the window would need to move back down closer to or at the standard window positioning.

If the addressing vehicle is the response device (RD) which should be attached to the letter with a micro-perf (a perforation with a high number of teeth used for laser sheets), the situation changes again. To work through the various scenarios, it is helpful, almost mandatory, that your designer have a basic knowledge of production issues (see **Key 10**).

Situation #2: Improper Positioning of Multi-Up Coupons Can Create Extra Costs

Another very common problem when printing stock to be used for laser personalization, is 1-up versus 'multi-up' RDs. Unless you have a designer who is adept enough to design a print-ready layout, these devices are normally created as a 1-up piece of artwork. The printer is then required to create the final 'multi-up' version that is required by the lettershop.

A printer who has expertise in dm production will provide <u>the necessary input </u>to avoid delays and extra costs.

A printer who is not familiar with laser imaging, or the subsequent insertion process, will not be aware of the potential problems should the RD be printed 1-up. At the very least, increased lasering costs are applicable. Since laser prices are based on a per-sheet rate, it stands to reason that it would be cheaper to laser 10,000 standard 3-up sheets than 30,000 non-standard 1-up sheets.

How To Design A Proper 3-Up RD Layout

To avoid laser programming issues in data preparation and trimming problems in the lettershop, it is best to make all three RDs exactly the same size on the sheet. On an 8-½ x 11 sheet, that would be an identical size of (11 ÷ 3 =) 3.67".

If the RD is a smaller size, all three should be justified toward the <u>top</u> and the left side of the sheet with the remaining waste positioned at the bottom and right of the sheet. There should be <u>no</u> gutter between the RDs unless they 'bleed' (ink runs off the edge) in which case you should allow at least a ¼" gutter for double trimming.

(Note that if the both the top and the bottom of the RD bleeds with the *same color*, it is not necessary to leave a gutter.)

Key 10: Use An Experienced Direct Mail Designer

> **Using a direct mail designer who is experienced with direct mail production techniques will save you time and money. It will be the cheapest money you'll ever spend.**

This is another biggie… it could almost be in first place.

I can't begin to emphasize how critical it is to use an art designer who is familiar with not only direct mail fundamentals but also with basic direct mail *production* techniques.

Aside from the fact that an inexperienced designer may affect your response rate with an unprofessional-looking package, using an experienced dm designer will at least make your job go through faster and in the worst case, it could save you <u>thousands of dollars</u> in extra costs.

Keep Your Mailing On Schedule With Properly Designed Artwork

If you are using one of your own staff (a common way to minimize costs), or even if you are doing it yourself, make sure you follow basic dm fundamentals as well as **proper design guidelines for printing**. Nothing can delay a mail date more quickly than waiting for revised artwork.

For example, a job may have been quoted as having an envelope with no 'bleeds' and running on a standard Jet Press (a special printing press for envelopes). However, when the artwork is checked, it is noted that the envelope has been designed 'bleeding' to the edges.

Now, a decision has to be made by the client – to stay with the bleeds at a much higher cost, or to revise the artwork. With any luck, if the client chooses the latter option, the printer may be able to make the change on the client's art by pulling back the bleeds. (Note: If a PDF, or **Portable Document Format**, has been provided for art, see **Key 1**.)

In another example, an experienced designer will allow for smaller-sized panels on a multi-page brochure that requires any inward-direction folding such as a roll-fold or double gatefold. Without designing specific panels with slightly smaller dimensions, the brochure will not fold properly.

One way for the printer to get around this problem is by trimming off a little bit of the end panel (only on certain folds) but care needs to be taken that nothing of consequence is being removed. Another way to avoid this particular folding issue is by using an accordian-fold, also called a Z-fold, where all panels are the same size.

But then again, the **lettershop** (see sidebar on next page) should be aware that a *friction-feeder* or *stream feeder* is required when this particular piece is being machine- inserted. (Note: A friction feeder is a special piece of equipment that is attached to an automated inserter to feed a multi-edged component onto the inserter track.)

Without getting into more details beyond the scope of this book, be aware that the use of friction-feeders must be carefully

---

Printers And Lettershops

Over the years, I have found that clients have different ideas of what a **dm printer** does.

From my perspective and throughout this ebook, I refer to a dm printer as one who provides *traditional print services to the dm industry*.

These services may include offset, web or letterpress with possible in-house bindery capabilities. I do not include **variable data printing (VDP)** such as laser printing in this mix.

These services are normally provided by **lettershops**, or mailing services companies.

However, some traditional printers or brokers provide VDP services and some lettershops choose not to provide them.

---

considered when multi-matching components are part of

your format. Direct mail art designers must be able to conceptualize how the finished product will be folded and inserted.

Let's now discuss one of the most important details of production – the addressing layout.

How To Lay Out The Address Block So It Will Show Properly In The Envelope Window

This is probably one of the most important production elements when designing a package format.

There are so many variables to consider here that it should suffice to say that only someone with a minimum of basic dm experience can do it properly, and even then it can be a toss-up. Some packages can be complicated production-wise.

The complexity of the production process increases tremendously when a format has been designed that does not lend itself well to standard dm production formats.

There will always be the 'award-winning' designer who has designed a 'creative' masterpiece that can only be processed manually (i.e. by hand) at great cost because production was an afterthought. If your production team is not in on at least one of your design team meetings (see **Key 6**), then it is very important, even mandatory, that your art designer be a dm design expert.

Bonus Key: Use Full-Color VDP For Better Response

> Direct mail designers and marketers recognize the fact that color *sells*. Color can make or break a campaign. Color, used with skill and understanding, has been shown to increase response.

VDP, or *variable data printing*, has actually been around for a long time. In its simplest form, it's been used since the late 1970s to personalize direct mail.

The equipment may have been more archaic but the fact that the data from one letter to the next changed means that it was *variable*. The term VDP became popularized when digital printing or *print-on-demand* (see sidebar) technology improved and became mainstream among marketers.

The original laser and inkjet printers focused mainly on black color, and even nowadays, most VDP in direct mail is still done using black toner only. That is because more specialized digital equipment is required to run additional colors, meaning more cost.

By now, you have probably received in your mailbox that impressive 4-color postcard from your favorite store - a piece that highlights your name in large white *knocked-out* type. And oddly enough, the photo on the card gives you that warm, fuzzy feeling.

That is because the image is *data-driven*, and has been selected especially for you based on your previous buying habits!

You are probably just one on a list of thousands or even millions, and yet the images printed for the person before or after you on the list may be completely different. And this is all done at incredible speed inline, with the consumer's personal data determining the image to be used.

Direct mail designers and marketers recognize the fact that color *sells*. In other words, as more color is added to the printed piece, the response rates tend to improve.

At the top end are the 4-color, graphic-intense variable mail

---

Print-On-Demand POD)

Printing process whereby documents can be printed as they are ordered, especially for single or low volumes that are impractical using traditional offset print methods. POD only became viable with digital printing.

Digital Printing Refers to printing from a *digital-based* image rather than traditional offset printing methods using plates. Output is done with special inkjet or toner digital presses. Ideal for short runs, quick turnaround and VDP. As technology improves, the gap between digital and traditional printing is narrowing.

Variable Data Printing (VDP)

A form of POD printing whereby text, graphics

Continued...

RAINER FISCHER

pieces that tend to open up your wallet more than any others.

Color can make or break a campaign. Color, used with skill and understanding, has been shown to increase response.

Dark versus light colors, contrast, color visual tricks – all these techniques in the right hands improve your chances of a successful campaign.

And at the end of it all, at the end of the production chain, are the printers, mailshops, lettershops and service providers with their vast range of presses, inkjet and toner printers who create the physical product which was once only a digital image on someone's computer.

Continued from previous sidebar…

or images are changed from one printed piece to the next without stopping. It is *one-to-one communication* in a mass production format. In its simplest form, VDP is simply called *personalization* where usually just name, address and a few other data-driven variables are changed. In its full-blown form, VDP changes complete images and graphics from one piece to the next. This kind of imaging requires special high-end digital equipment.

Such is the state of printing these days, with still more to come.

Summary of Secret Keys

#1: It is always advisable to provide 'native' art in its original design format to the printer. PDF-formatted art does not allow the printer to make any design changes at his end.

#2: Calculating 'overs' into your print order up front is a cheap insurance policy to allow for lettershop setup and spoilage as well as the occasional printer under-runs. Above all, refuse to work with any printers who specify an 'industry policy of 5% over or under.'

#3: Increasing the number of versions of offset-printed stock or laser 'shells' increases the risk for error during production. Whenever possible, use 'variable data printing' or personalization to minimize the number of printed versions.

#4: You can keep your imaging costs down by pre-printing (offset print) non-personalized areas of your letter. These areas include multiple pages and special techniques such as colored text, underlining, signatures and handwritten notes.

#5: Be careful what stock you plan to use for your direct mail campaign. It must be compatible for both the imaging equipment as well as the downstream insertion machines. The wrong stock can cause expensive delays and reprints.

#6: An excellent way to avoid costly delays is to take advantage of the expertise of your production suppliers prior to the actual production by having them sit in on design sessions.

#7: Scheduling the proper amount of time in your timetable for production will allow for the necessary quality control and 'buffer' time to accommodate unexpected delays

#8: Selecting the most appropriate supplier for your job is one of the most, if not **the** most, important parts of the production process. Building a solid relationship with the ideal supplier will ensure that your 'dream' jobs will not turn into nightmares.

#9: Using a printer who is experienced with direct mail production techniques will 'save your bacon' many times over. He will be a valuable partner by preventing minor issues from becoming major mistakes.

#10: Using a direct mail designer who is experienced with direct mail production techniques will save you time and money. It will be the cheapest money you'll ever spend.

Bonus Key: Direct mail designers and marketers recognize the fact that color *sells*. Color can make or break a campaign. Color, used with skill and understanding, has been shown to increase response.

Why Did I Write This Book?

Why did I write this book?

First of all, according to the *Direct Marketing Association*, almost 1/3 of the in-home cost of a direct mail campaign is the actual production. And, depending on the format of your package, up to 80% of the production cost can be **print production**.

Second of all, direct mail is more than just a three-legged stool: list, offer and copy. To make it really stable, you need the fourth leg called **production**. Unfortunately, in our fast-paced world of marketing, most of our campaign planning is usually spent on the first three legs. The fourth production leg becomes almost an afterthought.

While design, strategy, artwork and lists are all no doubt important, it would be foolish to consider the actual physical production as a foregone conclusion. In fact, during my many years in dm production, I learned one important rule – **the <u>simplest</u> direct mail campaign required the <u>greatest care</u>!**

Letting your guard at any time, **especially** for the 'easy' mailings, was leaving yourself open to potential disaster!

All the steps in the process of a direct mail campaign that come before the production are the *soft* services, like strategy, lists, copywriting and design.

These are services performed by humans. They are easy to understand.

But when it comes to the **hard** services like production, people get intimidated by all the new technology. This is especially true when it comes to printing presses which nowadays can refer to offset or digital printing. It gets further complicated when you're looking at *variable data printing* (VDP).

But unless you are a technician or operator of a high-end Heidelberg printing press or the latest Xerox digital printer, there is not really much hi-techiness (I don't think that's really a word but you get the idea) that you need to worry about as a direct mailer.

I'm here to tell you that you don't need to worry about all the nitty-gritty production details! Let's keep it SIMPLE.

So, from my 30+ years in the biz, I gathered up what I thought were the most commonly-asked questions and problem areas about dm production. I hear them over and over again. And if I don't hear about them, then I can *see* them - wrong stock, late stock, delayed drop dates, bad art design, incompetent vendors, etc.

So I've outlined the most common issues of direct mail production in this simple question-and-answer format. They are all important steps in the production process derived from my own experiences in producing over <u>thousands of mailings</u>.

They are 'real-life, hard-to-find, information-you-can-use' strategies. Incorporate as many of them as you can into ALL of your direct mail campaigns. The more you use, the less problems you will encounter in getting your mailing successfully into the hands of your target audience.

Your comments and questions are always welcome. Feel free to call me at **905.877.3656** or email me at rainer@dmgraphics.ca.

All The Best,

Rainer Fischer

P.S. Don't forget to check out the special offer (see below) which is exclusive to you as a thank you for being a purchaser of this book. But the offer is limited and won't be around forever, so you need to check it out ASAP.

About The Author: Rainer Fischer

Rainer Fischer has been actively involved in direct mail since 1980. He is a highly sought-after consultant and print management expert.

He is the founder of two successful direct mail companies where he developed he developed many systems to minimize direct mail production costs and, at the same time, maximize the client's ROI by employing unique production methods.

He is the 'secret weapon' of many veteran direct marketers for his ability to review a client's direct mail package <u>before</u> production and transform it into a 'direct mail-ready' format.

Among other direct marketing projects, he currently operates **DM Graphics Inc.**, a company specializing in direct mail printing and production services. He has continued to add to his knowledgebase through books, seminars and continued research into the production of direct mail. His websites at <u>www.dmgraphics.ca</u> and <u>www.directmailinsider.com</u> are valuable resources for dm printing and production.

To arrange a free consultation with Rainer to see how he may be able to assist your business or organization with its direct mail programs, call toll-free **1.866.365.3656**.

Now That You Have Read The Rest of This Book, Check Out A Very Special Direct Mail Offer That Is Only Available For A Limited Time!

http://specialoffer.dmgraphics.ca

Important Information

Please note that you have no copyrights to this publication and it is intended for your own personal use. You may not pass off this book as your own, or include it in any product or website without prior permission from the author.